THE ROUGH COLLIE

SHIEL

Illustrations by Sheila Smith

John Bartholomew & Son Limited
Edinburgh

First published in Great Britain 1981 by
JOHN BARTHOLOMEW & SON LIMITED
12 Duncan Street, Edinburgh EH9 1TA

ISBN 0 7028 8410 3
1st edition
Reprinted 1984

British Library Cataloguing in Publication Data

Shiel
   The Rough Collie. – (Bartholomew pet series).
   1. Collies
   I. Title   636.7'3   SF429.C6

Printed in Great Britain by
John Bartholomew & Son Limited, Edinburgh

Contents

Head of a Rough Collie

One: History

The Collie is accepted, even by non-Collie enthusiasts, as being, probably, the most beautiful of the canine species.

A dog of grace, a dog of much attraction yet, nevertheless, a thorough, working dog.

It is practically impossible to come up with the complete answer to the history of the breed. He must, I think, be the result of the intermixing of a variety of breeds or even of 'non-breeds' since the dog, in his early days, was bred entirely for his working ability. The first description of the dog as a Collie does not appear until well into the 19th century. Any farm dogs described before this date are distant from the Collie.

In Roman times, there were sheepdogs being used and we know from the bible (Job XXXI) that sheepdogs were tending the flocks. It is pretty certain that, during the times of the Roman invasion, their sheepdogs were introduced to Britain, since an army does not travel without its canines. These dogs, or their progeny, would surely stay in this country and, later, when the Britons suffered invasion from the Picts and Scots, certainly the dogs were plundered along with the cattle. The next step came of course, with the interbreeding of these dogs with the dogs they had at home. Sadly, there is no proof of this. Anyone can make a suggestion and no one suggestion is more likely to be correct than any other. It is interesting to surmise, but the only thing of which we can be certain is that any selection in the early days was solely for instinct and capabilities which gave the dog strong herding ability. Type, if there was type, would have been completely overlooked and no attention was paid to it until the last century, when dog shows first made their appearance and then it began to matter.

Of course, there would have been an overall *physical*

type, keeping the dog to a certain size, most suitable for his work.

The name, Collie, does not help either, since its origin is about as difficult as that of the dog itself. The word has been spelt in many ways, Coll, Colley, Coally and Coaly for example and, in Anglo-Saxon, the word *col* meant black and it is quite possible that the dog was so called after the black-faced sheep, which were very common in Scotland during those days.

No matter what he was called, he had a name by the end of the 18th century, and that name was 'Collie', which was to remain with him forever.

The Collie is one of the very oldest of the show dogs also. The first two shows held in Britain were confined to gundogs, but the third show, held in Birmingham in 1860, was for sporting and non-sporting dogs. At this show there was a class for sheepdogs. This meant that Collies, if any were exhibited, were put together with herding dogs, Bob-tails etc., and the only details we have of the winner was '1st – Mr Wakefield's bitch'. Most sad, that we know no more. Was she a Collie or something else? We shall never know.

From the records of early shows, we know that the sheepdog classes were always very popular, scheduled by most shows. The dogs appeared as Colleys, Sheepdogs or Collies, according to the whim of the Kennel

Rough Collie herding sheep

Club, but they quickly became divided into three groups, Rough-coated, Smooth-coated and Short-tailed. These latter were the Old English Sheepdog, which at that time was shown in competition with the Collie. It was not until 1895 that our breed was separated and had a permanent name as Collies (Rough) or Collies (Smooth). It was in 1870 that the breed finally settled into a name in the show classes, when a show at the Crystal Palace scheduled Sheepdogs Rough and Sheepdogs Smooth, so for the first time the breed was sub-divided by coat. Sad to relate the result in Smooths was shown as 'Dogs, Prize not awarded, want of merit'. A rather more frank comment than would be acceptable today in similar circumstances. In 1876, at a show in Ireland at Cork, the breed was scheduled as Colleys and two months later, in Brighton, they became Collies and from that moment the breed settled into this name by which they are known today.

During the first 10 years of the exhibition of Collies or Colley, no dogs appear to have made any impact on the breed and we had to wait until the 1870's for the first of 'The Greats' to arrive on the scene. Pride of place goes to the Old Cockie. Sadly, we have nothing but a photograph and that was taken after he was 10 years old. But there appears to be no doubt of his merit. By almost unanimous description, he was a really handsome animal. A rich sable, one of the early dogs of this colour and to him we owe every sable dog, world-wide, today. Cockie as he was also called, had a full white collar and the usual white markings, but his legs were spotted with sable, rather in the manner of the Cocker Spaniel. He was a sturdy, sound dog with a dense coat of excellent texture and he had a wonderful undercoat. Although we do not have his actual measurements, he was certainly not a big dog. It is recorded that his son Ch. Cocksie, was 'a little bigger than his sire' and we know that Cocksie was 21½ inches at the shoulder, so I imagine Cockie was certainly not more than 21 inches. Not only did he have an amazing show career, he had an incredible record as a sire. It is of special interest to note that he was very little used until he was eight years of age, what he could have done had he had a normal career is just impossible to imagine. He had no pedigree and his owner, Mr White, would never reveal where he had obtained him, so the start of all that is best in our breed as we know it today, will always be left in obscurity. Old Cockie was born in 1868 and died in 1882, a long life and one we certainly could not have done without.

Of the other dogs of this time, there are only a small handful which had any influence. There was Old Mec, who was a contemporary of Old Cockie, and many a battle they had in the show ring. Mec was a tricolour and, once again, had no pedigree. Scott was born in 1876 and was probably the best of Old Cockie's children. Sadly, this so very handsome dog was never shown because he was badly scalded as a youngster, but through his children he had a great influence, especially through his son Duncan, who became the grand-sire of Ch. Metchley Wonder.

Trefoil, again a dog without a pedigree, was born in 1873 and is the dog to which every single Collie, world-wide today, traces its pedigree. He had a wonderful show record, eclipsed by his success as a sire. He was tricolour and carried a coat of great length, but rather short of density, but he was a lovely shape and gay and attractive, with a fairly good head with an excellent eye and good ears. Here, then, are the dogs which founded the breed. Add to them the bitches Elsie, Ch. Madge and Old Bess and that is the beginning. One other dog deserves mention, because he had a great influence on the blue merles. This was Mr Brackenburg's Scott, born in 1873 and again without a pedigree. He was responsible for the glorious colour of the inmates of the first 'blue' kennel of merit, that of Mr Arkwright.

The blue merle colour, although it should have a chapter all to itself, must never be classed as separate from the other colours. All are Collies and it is quite wrong to separate them as happens in France, where they are awarded a separate set of C.Cs for this colour alone.

The blue merle was one of the commonest colours in the original sheepdogs. In the 19th century dogs of this colour were found in all parts of the country. In fact, they were so numerous and, in some cases so disliked, that many were destroyed at birth.

It is such a shame that the original name 'marled' became changed, for this word, a corruption of marbled, exactly describes the required markings, while merle means a blackbird!

A blue merle should be clear silvery blue, dappled with black, which is never in large patches. It may carry the usual markings as in the other colours, and should always have bright tan markings in the places in which one finds them on the tricolour. The eyes can be brown, blue, either or both, or part of either or both.

The blue merle is a modification of black, thanks to the presence of the dilution factor, and to the pigmentation granules in each hair being less numerous than in the dog of whole colour. It is also due to the fact that the granules are arranged in a certain pattern in each hair. For this reason the true blue merle is very difficult to breed to perfection and because of this it presents a great challenge to those who try.

The blue merle colour can only happen when one parent is blue. The *blue* merle pattern cannot appear unless the bi-colour pattern is also present, for the dilution factor must work on the bi-colour to produce blue merles. The bi-colour is the black and tan pattern.

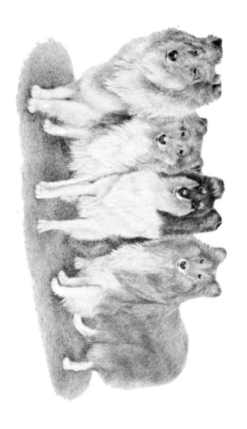

Blue Merles (*left*), black (*centre*) and sable (*right*) Rough Collies

Because of the destruction of the blue puppies in the early days, this colour was almost never seen in the ring and if it had not been for a few dedicated breeders concentrating on the colour, we should surely be without blue merles, loveliest of colours, in the ring today.

It was in the latter part of the 19th century that the resuscitation came about. Mr Arkwright was most certainly the man most dedicated to the task. His kennel was disbanded as long ago as 1890 but he had the most outstanding blue merles, of most gorgeous colour which has rarely been equalled today. He held that one should always mate merles to tricolours to produce *good* blues, but that the *best* blues came from using black and tan partners. We cannot do this since there are no black and tan Collies today. In his opinion one should never use a sable as a partner, since this gave muddy coloured merles and blue-eyed sables, as we have found in our own day, but occasionally he had to do this since, in his day, sables were by far superior in type. Today all the colours are equally good in type, so I see no reason why we need use sables in our breeding programme. The mating of merle and merle is sometimes indulged in, often with great success, but there is always the danger of producing defective puppies, wholly or partly white puppies which may be deaf or blind, or both, and if carried to extremes they may be born with deformed eyes or no eyes at all. It you mate merle to merle giving three of four merle grandparents, you are playing with fire, yet it can produce winners. A blue-eyed white of such a mating, if it is not deaf, will almost certainly produce, when mated to a tricolour, puppies of excellent colour.

The start of the blues in the show ring is fairly clear. The first sire of any value was Mr Brackenburg's Scott, recorded at the Kennel Club as grey, tan and white, with china eyes, but Mr Arkwright described him as 'the perfect blue merle colour'. He was a very typical dog, who did his share of winning. Mr Arkwright mated his bitch Russet to him. Russet is described as a red sable and a red grizzle and it is certain that she was a sable merle. But whatever her colour, this mating laid the foundations of the blue merle colour in the early days. Ch. Blue Ruin, a most lovely bitch, won the Collie Club Trophy for best of breed when she was four years of age, in 1888, and so became the first blue merle ever to reach the top in open competition against the other colours. Mr Arkwright was not the only one to find interest in this colour. He quickly found competition from Messrs Doyle, Boddington and Power, until the auction sale of his Collies on April 17th, 1890. The dogs were dispersed all over Britain.

Two: The Standard

The first standard for the Collie was drawn up in 1881 and revised in 1898 and 1910. In 1950, for the first time, the Kennel Club published, unofficially, the standard for every breed so, in that year, a further revised standard came into being. From that date it became impossible to alter any standard, even in the tiniest respect, without K.C. permission, and then there is no chance unless the majority of the breed clubs agree.

In the late 1950's, it was felt that our standard needed amplification and clarification and some 10 years were spent obtaining agreement between the clubs, of which there were 15, until, in February 1969, the Kennel Club finally approved the revised standard. This was the most important thing which has happened to the Collie in the last 50 years.

Standard of the Collie
Reproduced by permission of the Kennel Club

Characteristics: *To enable the Collie to fulfil a natural bent for sheepdog work its physical structure should be on lines of strength and activity, free from cloddiness and without any trace of courseness. Expression, one of the most important points in considering relative values, is obtained by the perfect balance and combination of skull and foreface, size, shape, colour and placement of eye, correct position and carriage of ears all harmoniously blended to produce that dreamy yet alert outlook which makes the perfect Collie the most beautiful of the canine race.*

General Appearance: *The Collie should instantly appeal as a dog of great beauty, gifted with intelligence, alertness and activity. With no part out of proportion to the whole he should stand with impassive dignity and his movements, governed by perfect anatomical formation, should*

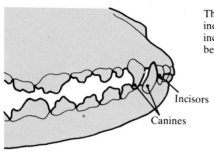

The correct 'scissors bite'. The upper incisors fit closely over the lower incisors and the upper canines fit behind the lower canines.

Incisors

Canines

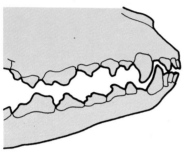

'Pincer' or 'Level bite'. Teeth of the upper jaw meet the teeth of the lower jaw.

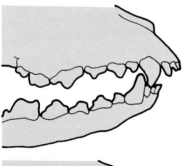

'Overshot'. The top jaw protrudes over the lower, causing a space. The canines are in reverse positions.

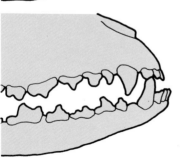

'Undershot'. The lower incisors protrude beyond the upper jaw, causing a space between the upper and lower canines.

be smooth and graceful. An abundance of coat, mane and frill with shapeliness of head and sweetness of expression all combine to present a pleasing and elegant picture that will inspire and secure admiration.

Head and Skull: *The skull should be flat and moderately wide between the ears with a gradual tapering towards the eyes, the width depending upon the combined length of skull and muzzle, the whole to be considered in connection with the size of the dog. The muzzle continues in an almost unbroken line towards the nose and must not show weakness or be snipy or lippy. Below the eyebrow there should be a slight and perceptible, but not prominent, stop which brings the bridge of the nose line slightly below the surface line of the skull. Whatever the colour of the dog the nose must be black.*

Eyes: *Are a very important feature, and give expression to the dog. They should be of medium size, set somewhat obliquely, of almond shape and of dark brown colour except in the case of merles, when the eyes are frequently (one or both) blue and white or china; expression full of intelligence, with a quick alert look when listening.*

Ears: *Should be small and moderately wide at the base, and placed not too close together on top of the skull nor too much to the side of the head. When in repose they should be usually carried thrown back, but when on the alert brought forward and carried semi-erect, with tips slightly drooping in attitude of listening.*

Mouth: *The teeth should be of good size, with the lower incisors fitting closely behind the upper incisors, a very slight space not to be regarded as a serious fault.*

Neck: *Should be muscular, powerful, of fair length, and somewhat arched.*

Forequarters: *The shoulders should be sloped. The forelegs should be straight and muscular, neither in nor out at elbows, with a fair amount of bone; the forearms somewhat fleshy, with pasterns showing flexibility without weakness.*

Points of the Rough Collie

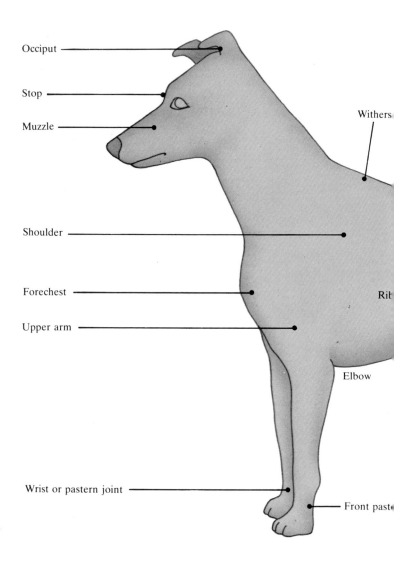

Occiput

Stop

Muzzle

Withers

Shoulder

Forechest

Rib

Upper arm

Elbow

Wrist or pastern joint

Front past

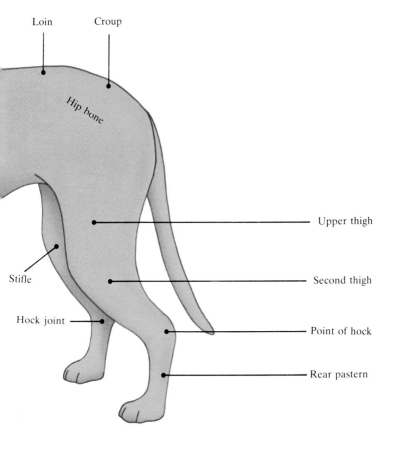

Loin

Croup

Hip bone

Upper thigh

Stifle

Second thigh

Hock joint

Point of hock

Rear pastern

19

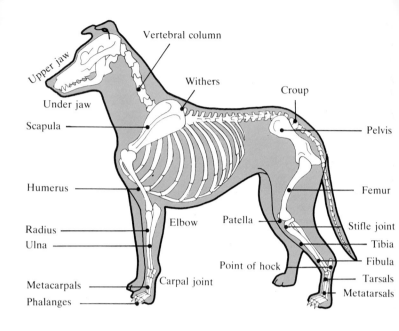

Body: *Should be rather long with well-sprung ribs, chest deep, fairly broad behind the shoulders.*

Hindquarters: *Loins slightly arched and powerful. The hind legs should be muscular at the thighs, clean and sinewy below the hocks with well-bent stifles.*

Feet: *Should be oval in shape, soles well padded, and the toes arched and close together. The hind feet less arched, the hocks well let down and powerful.*

Tail: *The tail should be moderately long, carried low when the dog is quiet, with a slight upward 'swirl' at the end, and may be gaily carried when the dog is excited, and not over the back.*

Coat: *Should be very dense, the outer coat harsh to the touch, the inner or under coat soft, furry , and very close, so close as almost to hide the skin. The mane and frill should be very abundant, the mask or face smooth, as also the ears at the tips, but they should carry more hair* *towards the base; the forelegs well feathered, the hind legs above the hocks profusely so; but below the hocks fairly smooth, although all heavily coated Collies are liable to grow a slight feathering. Hair on the brush very profuse.*

Colour: *Colour and markings are immaterial, but other points being equal, a nice showily marked dog is preferred.*

Weight and size: *Dogs, 22 – 24 in [55½ – 61 cm] at the shoulders. Bitches, 20 – 22 in [50 – 55½ cm] Dogs 45 lb to 65 lb [20½ – 29½ kg]. Bitches, 40 lb to 55 lb [18 – 25 kg].*

Faults: *Length of head apparently out of proportion to the body and head of the Borzoi type are to be strongly condemned. Weak, snipy muzzle; overshot mouth; heavy or gooseberry-coloured eyes, and glassy staring eyes are very objectionable. Domed skull, high-peaked occiput, prominent cheek, dish-faced or Roman nosed. Body flat-sided, short or cobby. Weak long pasterns, out at elbows, crooked forearms. Cow-hocks, straight hocks. Large, open, flat, or hare feet; feet turned outwards or inwards. Tail short or carried over the back, or twisted to one side. A soft, silky, or wavy coat, or insufficient under-coat.*

Now you have read the standard you should have a reasonable idea of what is required in the Collie. You will readily see that we want a head of great smoothness, and very well balanced, but at the same time having a well-rounded strong muzzle, with jaws which show no weakness, particularly the underjaw. It seems as if some of our breeders and judges today are forgetting these points, for Collies appear, and win, in the show ring, which have almost 'beaks' instead of strong, well rounded muzzles. The eye gives expression to the dog and the standard demands a 'sweet' expression. This one word was just about the only alteration made to the paragraph on eyes, but it has made all the difference in setting out just exactly what is required. Any change from the accepted shape, placement and size of the eye is very important. A Collie with a round, square-set eye can only see directly in front, unless the eyes are set on the side of the head, which ruins the expression.

Ears should be tipped over, by one-third. Thus a guide line has been set up for judges who have found it difficult to decide just how much should be tipped.

We expect the neck to be well arched, which is quite essential in giving to the breed its proud appearance.

The fact that the body is 'a trifle long, when compared to the height', gives a definite picture of the actual length required, and the fact that the standard definitely calls for a back which is 'firm, with a slight rise over the loin' gives no excuse for passing a 'sway-back' which, in the past, did happen from time to time.

The standard asks for well let-down hock and adds the word 'powerful'. The position of the hock is extremely important, for a dog in which the hock is placed too high, cannot get his hind legs well under his body to enable him to produce the strong drive from the rear, which is essential for his shepherd work.

The description of the gait is quite excellent, describing the movement exactly as we wish to see it. The same remarks apply to the description of the tail. However, one so frequently sees, taking the highest awards in the show ring, dogs which carry their tails very high, even over their backs, that sometimes one wonders whether the judges ever read the standard!

The description of the coat is also excellent, demanding one which 'fits' the dog, not wanting one which 'stands-off'. The correctly fitting coat finishes the picture of the Collie, where the coat runs smoothly back, sweeps down over the loin to the joint of the tail and stresses the flowing lines needed in the correct hind-quarters.

Three: The Stud Dog

The management of the stud dog is something very special. I do not mean that his maintenance is difficult to keep him in condition, he does not require any special treatment, but by management I mean the way in which he is handled during the actual mating.

The dog must have some very important attributes before he can seriously be considered as a stud dog. He must have an excellent pedigree which contains the bloodlines which have played and are still playing, an important part in improving the breed. This pedigree should be strong for many more generations than appear on the usual five generation pedigree form. You have to be as sure as you can that for 8 or 10 generations there are no really weak spots. A weak spot means that the bloodline goes back to a line known not to have produced really top class stock, on either the male or the female side. More often you will find that the pedigree fails on the dam's side. This, of course, is because earlier breeders have been trying to improve their lines by stepping up in the use of a stud dog. It is on the female side that your danger will possibly lie.

The potential stud dog must come of stock quite free of inherent tendencies to any particular disease or constitutional weakness, quite apart from whether he is a good show specimen or not. To be of any real economic value, and this has to be considered, he must be of value in the show ring as well. For without successes there will not be a demand for his services. He must also be of excellent temperament, for the shy dog is the greatest possible detriment to the breed. He must be a 'male' and have no trace of femininity and he must be capable, sensible and virile in his work.

The Collie, being a medium-sized breed, should not be used too young, but on the other hand you should not

wait until he is too old because it is often difficult to start an older dog. I think it is ideal for a Collie to mate his first bitch at about 10 months of age; he should not then have any more bitches until he is about 16 months old and, from then on, until the age of around 2 years, he should not really have more than one bitch per month, but because these things are seasonal we often cannot choose.

The young dog should be trained from the very beginning in the way you intend to use him always, and you will find that it is saving of time and of his energies if you hold his bitches for him. For the first time it is essential to use an older bitch. One who is experienced, flirtatious and known to be easy to mate should be used. The worst thing that can happen to the dog is to fail to mate at his first attempt; it will make him uneasy, lose condition and later, when asked to try again, he may well have lost confidence. If that first bitch really teaches him what to do, your problems will be largely overcome.

It is advisable to have two people helping on the first

occasion at least, one to hold the bitch's head, the other to help the dog.

They should be introduced to one another on a leash, so that you can be sure she is really ready and she may then flirt with him a little. If she seems happy about it, they should be taken to the place where, for ever after, you intend carrying out the matings. Here they can be released for a few minutes if you so wish, but do not let the play continue for too long, the dog will tire himself. Be as certain as you possibly can that the bitch will not snap at the dog, if there is any doubt then she should be muzzled with a bandage. A bite, at this stage, might well put the dog off for many months. As soon as the bitch has shown she is ready and quite willing to stand firmly, she should be held by the head and the dog allowed to mount.

As she does so, the bitch should be held from underneath by the second assistant. This must be done without any fuss and certainly without getting in the dog's way. Slightly raise the vulva to make it easier for the dog to enter. The easiest way to do this is to sit on the ground beside the bitch, on her left-hand side and place your left hand flat, under the bitch, from the side and then backwards between her hind legs, with the vulva just lying between the first and second fingers of the hand. Placed like this the exact place of the penis can be felt and the dog given every possible help. As soon as the dog has entered, he will start to work very rapidly, then the right arm can be passed behind him and he can be held in position until the 'tie' takes place. Even a bitch who has previously been mated will usually whimper slightly during the swelling of the penis and it is a good thing at this time to talk reassuringly to both the bitch and the dog, for he may fear he has done something wrong if the bitch is crying under him. Be sure to tell him how clever he is. When the 'tie' is completed the dog will get off the bitch, then turn around. He should be helped in this, for any chance of pulling away must be avoided, for this can cause rupture to the dog and/or irreparable harm to the bitch. I find the best way to turn a dog is to hold both animals' tails in one hand, leaving the other free to help the dog get his leg over, if this is necessary.

The 'tie' needs some explanation. The dog is the only species of mammal in which such a thing takes place. All other mammalians are equipped with Cowper's glands, which eject semen in a swift emission as soon as the vagina is penetrated. Since the dog is without these glands he can only emit semen slowly on a drip principle so the absence of Cowper's glands is offset by the 'tie'. As soon as the penis enters the vagina it begins to swell gradually until, in about its centre, there is a very pronounced bulbous swelling which makes it impossible for the dog to retract without doing very serious damage. To make things even more sure, while the penis is swelling, the muscles of the bitch contract around it, holding it firmly and the length of time of this muscular contraction determines the length of the 'tie'. So the length varies from bitch to bitch, and is not always the same, even with the same dog. The average length of a 'tie' is about 15 – 20 minutes but it can last well over an hour, and there is nothing you can do to hurry things up! During the 'tie' the bitch should not be allowed to sit down, nor fidget etc., and the dog should be watched all the time. Both dogs can be held gently if necessary.

The young stud dog may resent the bitch being held at the rear. If so he must be allowed, for the first mating, to go about matters in his own manner, but the moment he penetrates he should be held as described above and, at the same time, put your left hand under the body as described so that he may become accustomed to it for the next time. A great deal of time can well be spent, and *should* be spent on the first mating for much time will be saved on later matings if he has a difficult bitch to cope with.

You must remember that, probably, the young dog, being used for the first time, will probably emit semen in which the sperm is dead and so such a mating should always be a dual one. The second ejaculation is likely to be fertile, as the old, dead sperm will have been passed out and for this reason it is always wise, even essential, to give a second service. The same remarks apply if the dog has not been used for some time but, with these two exceptions, there is rarely need for two services.

The stud fee for your dog should be agreed upon before the mating takes place. The dog who is already established as a stud, will have his fee already settled, but the one mating his first bitch presents a slight problem. The fee you are going to charge must be stated, for the fee for any dog is paid *for the service,* and not for the *result* of the service. But this is not quite fair for the maiden dog. It is, I think, best to say that you will take either a puppy, or the fee you have set, when the bitch whelps. By such an arrangement no one loses. But be quite sure to get this arrangement set out in writing. Other than this, the fee is always payable at the time of mating, unless other arrangements have been made, and these too must always be in writing.

Sometimes you are asked if you will take a puppy instead of a fee to a proved dog, and the owner of the bitch should not feel that it casts any slur on his bitch's merits, if the owner of the dog cannot agree to such a request. There is nothing more awkward to the owner of a kennel than to be left with just one puppy at a different age from anything else in the kennel; it is for this reason that it may be necessary to say 'no'.

Although the stud fee is payable for the service and not for its result, most owners say that, should no puppies result, then there will be a free service next time provided the dog is still in your ownership. This is not compulsory, but is just a 'gentleman's agreement'.

A dog placed at public stud should have at least one live litter to his credit. He should have a stud card, which sets out his colour, possibly a photograph, his fee, his stud book or registration number and his pedigree, preferably to five generations. It must also carry your name, address and phone number. It is wise to have a little clause which says that every care will be taken of a visiting bitch, but that no responsibility can be accepted. This may save you a great deal of trouble should an accident occur.

Finally, make sure that your stud dog is fit and well and absolutely free of all parasites.

Four: Breeding a Litter

Everyone who has a Collie arrives at the moment when they feel they would like to breed a litter. If their Collie is a bitch there is not much problem. However, if it is a male, things must be changed.

Seeking a good bitch will not be too easy, since a good one is usually likely to cost high, or else is not for sale at any price. If you have decided to attend several shows, in order to see what stock may be available, or to visit a number of kennels with the same object in view, you will find a big divergence in type from kennel to kennel. Once you have decided which type appeals to you most (and remember that a number of different types can all be correct and fall within the standard), then you must concentrate on the kennels which have that type.

However, you must decide, before setting about breeding, whether you can afford to raise a litter. The puppies must be well-fed, as must their dam, and this, today, costs a great deal of money. If you feel that it will make a drain on your resources then you should not be tempted, because puppies must have the best possible start in life. It is no good 'skimping' or feeding second best. Your future winners are made or marred in these first weeks and months.

Probably the best way of obtaining a good bitch is to obtain her on breeding terms from her original owner. This is a method by which you may pay a 'cut price' for the bitch, but she remains, for her first litter, in the name of the original owner. Then, when she has puppies, these are shared on a basis that will have been previously agreed. The terms and arrangements for the sharing of the litter have to be firmly decided, and *always* in writing, and these must be strictly adhered to. The details will vary according to the age and quality of the bitch and also according to the kennel from which she comes. You never need to accept the offer if you do not wish to do so and you can 'shop around' to see who will make you the best offer. However, probably the biggest advantage of this method of obtaining your bitch is that, when you are satisfactorily fixed up with her, you should have all the knowledge and experience of the kennel owner to fall back on. Such a person will obviously want you to do the best you can and will almost certainly choose the stud dog to which the bitch will be mated. This you must agree to and anyway almost certainly the choice will be good, probably better than you can make yourself. In the agreement which is drawn up there will surely be a clause covering the loss of the bitch before the terms of the agreement are fulfilled and another, which states that, on completion of the terms of the agreement, the bitch becomes unconditionally your property. Although the bitch has remained in the original owner's name you are still allowed to register, with your kennel-name, your share of the puppies. I am sure you will find that you will obtain helpful advice on the rearing of the litter also, because the owner will want the puppies she has to be well-reared. Then remember that, if all has gone well, you have, forever, someone you can fall back on for advice.

Many Champions have been bred from bitches acquired in this way. In fact, my own first Champion Collie was so acquired, though in that particular instance I was allowed to choose the stud dog.

Take into careful consideration the pros and cons of each way of starting your kennel, then go ahead and do what you think is likely to be best for you.

Let us imagine now that your bitch has reached the age when you expect her to come into season and be ready for mating. In the first place, don't imagine that, because she is nine months you can expect the season to happen. The book tells us that bitches come in at that age, but the Collies never seem to read the books. She may well wait until she is 15 months or more before she shows any signs. However, it is not too early to make arrangements with the owner of the stud dog. Provided you are free to make the choice yourself, that is, if you have not obtained your bitch on breeding terms, then you should have decided well in advance the dog you consider the ideal partner. Study her pedigree most carefully and, by asking around, find out all you can about her ancestors. As a newcomer to the breed, you cannot be expected to know how the antecedents looked, but you can certainly find out. Further, try to discover whether there is, in her pedigree, a really good male, who has proved himself prepotent for those characteristics for which he is most admired. If he is still alive, and still producing puppies, weigh up the possibilities of putting your bitch back to him. If he can no longer be used, but you still want what is good from him, try to find a good son of his or a double grandson who excels in the points you want and who, if possible, has proved that he can produce these points also.

Contact the stud dog owner telling him when you expect your bitch to be in season, and make a tentative booking for her. Then, the moment she comes in, contact him again, tell him the actual day she started and the day you propose bringing her to be mated.

So far, I have not told you the signs of the bitch being in season. Usually the first sign is a very slight, but thickish, whitish discharge from the vagina. If you have a male around he will probably tell you when she is starting, specially if he is a young inexperienced fellow. The older dogs have more sense! Within a day or two the discharge will gradually colour until it is red. Dogs are *supposed* to have an appreciable swelling of the vulva, something which happens in most breeds and all the books tell us to expect this, but this is not usually so with

The genital organs

Dog

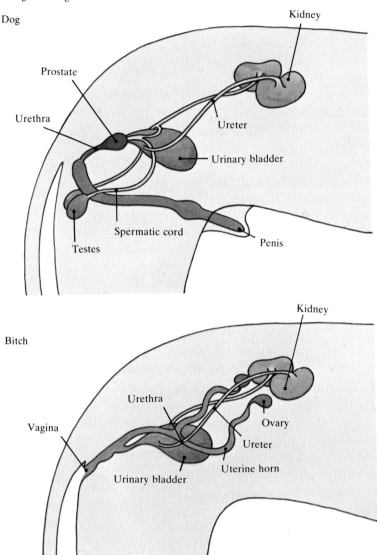

Bitch

the Collie, there is rarely any swelling at all. I have frequently had bitches booked to my dogs, only to be phoned the night before and told, 'It's no use coming, she hasn't swollen at all and will never get mated'. You can completely forget this in our breed and she will almost certainly be quite easy to mate.

The bitch herself will probably indicate when she is ready. This she does by raising her tail. She will do this when confronted with a dog, often for another bitch, if she is rubbed gently on the back just above the root of her tail, or if the vulva is gently touched. She does not fly her tail over her back, as with a 'gay' tail, but she lifts it quite stiffly from the root, and flicks it directly sideways, so that it sticks out at about an angle of 45 degrees before dropping down with its natural weight. When rubbed or sniffed by another dog, she will move her tail, still in the same position, from side to side; this is the moment for mating.

Every stud dog owner has his own method of handling his dog, as I have explained in the chapter on the stud dog, and to his methods you must acquiesce. The owner may offer you a second service probably the following day, but in my opinion, unless the first mating was an unsatisfactory one, there is no need for a repeat in a dog that is frequently used. It is easy to appreciate that the owner of a dog which is in much demand and used frequently, will not be anxious to give a second service, because of the risk of overusing the dog. A popular dog, during the season (and these things do run in seasons) may well mate four bitches a week, and if everyone wanted two services the poor dog would never have any time off! It is good to allow the bitch to rest a while before she starts her return journey, unless she is absolutely used to a car and it does not worry her at all. She must, of course, be kept under surveillance for the remainder of her season, usually another one and a half weeks, as she was in the beginning, for a bitch, once mated, may well be mated by another dog and conceive to him as well, so there can be no guarantee of the paternity of the puppies.

For the first four weeks after mating there is no need to treat the bitch differently in any way. During this time it is very difficult to know whether she is in whelp or not. You may notice she has an erratic appetite, on her food one day, off the next and, if she is a bitch you know really well, you may spot some slight change in her character. She may alter her habits or her personality very slightly, and this you will see more clearly in a 'house-pet' than in one who lives in a kennel. At a time between the 25th and 28th days after mating (and these times are important) your veterinary surgeon may be able to tell you if she is in whelp or not and, if she is, from this time on, she needs extra attention. Her way of life should not be altered at all; her exercise, provided it was adequate in the first place, should be neither diminished nor augmented, but food is the important item for the remaining five weeks, when she may be carrying as many as eight or nine, even more, puppies, and she must be helped in every way possible, to make a good job of it, with the least possible strain on herself. Collies are usually exceptionally good mothers, but they carry this too far, becoming very self-sacrificial and if she is not properly fed, she will almost certainly drain her own body to give to her puppies.

As soon as you are sure she is in whelp, her diet must be altered. I consider the ideal diet for a pregnant bitch is as follows:

Breakfast : Cereals or wholemeal bread, with 1 pint of milk. A raw egg, if possible, should be added daily. She should also receive the appropriate number of Canoval or SA37 tablets.

Mid-day : 1 – 1½ lb [454 – 681 g] raw meat (lean).
6.00 p.m. : As mid-day.
10.00 p.m.: A bowl of biscuit meal soaked in boiling stock or milk.

The bitch will probably not take to this change immediately but will require a day or two to adjust. Accustom her to it by giving her two meals on the first day, increase the size of the meat meal on the second, and offer the fourth meal on the third day. By the end of four or five days she should be quite happy.

Don't worry if she misses a meal, or even all her meals for one day, but don't let it become a habit. If she gets fussy, vary the diet. Stay with the raw meat if possible, but this can be varied. Mutton makes a tasty change from beef or horse, also she can have fish for a change. If necessary, try lightly cooking the meat for one meal and offering it raw for the next. Rabbit or chicken will almost always tempt her, but if you are stuck with a problem it is up to you to solve it. Use your ingenuity, ring the changes until you find something really tempting. It is rare that an 'in-whelp' bitch is a bad doer, but these suggestions may be of help. I had one particular bitch who had a different 'fad' every time she was in whelp. For the first litter, everything had to have cheese sauce on it, for her second she would not look at cheese, but everything had to have a rabbit flavour – mind you, I am quoting an extreme case, I do not believe in pandering to a dog except a bitch in whelp but, if you get a choosey one, you must do all you can.

Beyond keeping your bitch really well fed, and with a constant supply of *fresh* drinking water, there is only her exercise to think about. During the early days she should have as much unrestricted exercise as she wants. She must never be forced to go for a walk on a leash. She will carry on just as usual, chasing birds or galloping about. Do not make any change at all, except if she is exercised with other dogs and they are a bit rough, and likely to knock her about. If this is so, then, after the end of the seventh week, she should just be exercised with an old, staid Collie. Some people only exercise during the last two weeks on a leash. This, I do not agree with. Firstly it is much more tiring to be exercised on a leash than free because she must adjust to our pace and also, if she is a willing bitch, she will not want to hang back and appear not to want to go, but free she can easily assert herself and indicate it's time to go home!

There is just one more thing to do in the prepuppy days and this is to prepare a whelping box. First you must decide where she is to have her puppies, on this depends the type of box you will need. If, as I think is usual, she will have them in a room in the house and there is central heating in it, she may well need no additional heating and she can have an open box. If she is to whelp in a cold corner she will need a box with infra-red heating and a box which has a removable lid. Let us start with this one. The box will need to be about $3 \times 4 \times 2\frac{1}{2}$ feet [$90 \times 120 \times 75$ cm] high. It is preferable that the whole of the 4 ft [120 cm] side should not be open, but a hole made in it, about 6 in [15 cm] from the ground and about 2 ft [60 cm] wide. A thick blanket should hang from the top, completely covering this opening, but be quite sure it does not touch the floor, so that the bitch can get in and out as she wishes. This makes a dark place, not too unlike the place she would have chosen if it had been left to her. Also, in such a box, every scrap of heat given off by the bitch and her babies, is conserved, so that the babies can live in a fairly high temperature. However, such arrangements are rarely adequate for the first few days after birth. Most newborn puppies which die, do so from chilling and it is most difficult to resuscitate a puppy once it has become thoroughly chilled. Remember that they have been in a temperature of

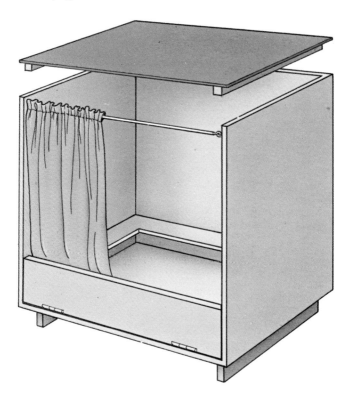

101.5°F at least and are suddenly shot into the cold world where the temperature will only be, at best, about 25°F lower. Almost certainly, except for puppies born in the height of summer, you will need to remove the lid of the box and hang over it an infra-red lamp. *Never* use a white light, because this worries the bitch and can well affect her eyes and the eyes of the babies. I prefer a red bulb, because this gives sufficient light to work by and does not worry anyone, but if you prefer it, you can use a 'dull emitter', which gives you the same result but without any light. You must make sure that the lamp is not too close, since then you will dehydrate the bitch as well

37

as, possibly, making the pups too warm. If the babies lie under the lamp close together, but not squashed in a tight ball, then you have the lamp about right. You must also remember that newborn puppies do not have any 'shivering mechanism', the muscles which produce shivering are not yet advanced enough to work and it will be some little time, about two weeks I believe, before the babies can shiver which helps to warm them.

However, there is, today, a new product on the market which is used as a whelping bed. This is 'Vet-Bed', a cover which looks a bit like a sheepskin rug but, being man-made, it washes and then dries most easily and gives all the heat necessary for the babies. However, I have had so many bitches who would not have any bedding in her box, not even newspaper, that you must be prepared for such a thing happening to you.

It is an accepted scientific fact that quite a lot of the

food eaten by your bitch is used simply to keep up body temperature. So all food fed to your bitch should be warm, to lessen the time the body will take after a meal to return it to its correct heat. During the time the temperature is down, growth of the puppies virtually stops, so since you are now feeding four times each day, this can add up to quite a time.

I do not think it necessary to have a guard rail inside a whelping box for a Collie. When I have lost any puppies from being squashed this has happened away from the edges, so I have never used a rail, but if you would feel safer with one then this should be placed all round the box, about 4 in [10 cm] from the floor and about 3 – 4 in [7 – 10 cm] away from the walls. This prevents a puppy being squashed behind the bitch.

If you are not using a Vet-Bed in your box, then by far the best bedding is several thicknesses of newspaper. The bitch, before whelping, will rip up her bedding anyway and the newspaper can be replaced as often as you wish. Straw and hay should *never* be used. Straw, because not only can a puppy get lost in it, but also straw can prick the eye of a newborn baby and cause damage, even blindness. Hay is not good because it frequently carries lice and also the pups can get lost in it. Woodwool is safe with regard to eye damage, but there is still the risk of getting lost.

The time for puppies to be born is 63 days after the day of mating, or so say the books! However, especially for maiden bitches, you can expect the puppies from around the 58th day. The best tip I can give you is, starting a week before she is due, to take her temperature twice daily. This is a most sure guide and may well save you trouble. The bitch's temperature, about 24 hours before she starts in labour, drops to around 98°F. I have known it to go even lower. It stays around that temperature for about 18 hours, then it goes back up, probably to about 100°F a few hours before the great event takes place. It is very unusual to have a bitch whose temperature hardly drops at all. Another sign is that the bitch urinates frequently, only a drop or two, but she does it much more often than normal. Then she will become very restless and at this stage she should be taken to her whelping area. There she will start to make her bed, tearing up her paper, if you are using it. It is unlikely she will tear up a Vet-bed, since this is practically indestructible! She may go on doing this for many hours before reaching the next stage. At this time she can be left alone, just look in hourly to keep your mind at rest.

When labour truly begins she becomes more and more restless, pants incessantly and has very quick breathing. She will also turn around, look at and lick her tail. Sometimes the first arrival emerges as soon as the pains begin, on others they may continue for some time before the birth. However, if the bitch continues straining for about two hours with nothing happening, then you should contact your veterinary surgeon. She will strain very hard during this period, but she also has times of rest between.

There is no doubt at all that most bitches like to have their owners present during the actual whelping. She probably will not require any help at all but I'm certain your presence will give her confidence.

Occasionally, you get a bitch who must whelp where she chooses. This may even be in your lap, but you'll have to grin and bear it, for nothing will change her mind. I know a bitch who carried this to such a point that, when she was removed from her chosen spot (the drawing room sofa!) she turned off her whelping mechanism when she was put in the bathroom and did it repeatedly and to such an extent that her whole litter was born dead.

Collies are, as a rule, excellent mothers and very easy

whelpers and you really do not need to expect any problems, but if a puppy gets held up because it is too large or wrongly presented, or for some other reason, that puppy, of course, stops the arrival of those which follow, and any hold-up may mean death.

When the labour pains really start, immediately turn on the heater in the box.

The first thing you will notice is a greenish discharge, then quite soon, the membraneous water-bag protruding from the vulva. Each puppy with one exception, arrives in its own sac. The one exception is that, very, very occasionally, two puppies may share a sac, they are known as free-martins and are always sterile.

Do not try to help her at this moment, just watch. If all is normal one of two things happen, either the bitch will rip the bag, letting the fluid escape, to be followed almost at once by the whole puppy, or else the puppy suddenly arrives still enclosed in its sac. The bitch should then immediately rip the sac open and lick up the fluid. The puppy is still attached to the placenta or after-birth and mum will immediately bite and sever the umbilical cord, then eat the after-birth. This done (it takes but a matter of seconds), she will immediately turn her attention to the puppy, licking, often quite roughly, until it breathes and gives its first cry.

Occasionally, with a first litter, when the first puppy is born, mother is bewildered and doesn't know what to do. Then it's up to you to do it for her and do it quickly. Grab the puppy, slit the bag, which though tough, can be broken with the fingers, and the puppy will fall from the bag. Take a quick look to make sure there is no mucous in the mouth then give it to mother, holding it to her muzzle. She will probably begin to lick it at once, but if not then rub it very briskly in a Turkish towel. The pup will almost certainly yell and mother will equally certainly demand you give it to her and your troubles are over. As soon as her instinct is aroused she will carry on and finish the job herself. However, stay with her, she will want you to do so, and if you leave an accident may happen and a puppy become suffocated.

Quite often a baby will be born but will still be attached to the after-birth, which is retained inside the dam. In such a case, make quite sure that it appears, there is no need to sever the umbilical cord at this stage, but wait until the after-birth appears. It is especially important to see it arrive if it is the last after-birth. It is not always easy to see each after-birth appear, because it is the instinctive action of the dam to eat it. I always allow my bitches to do this. This was a provision of nature to provide nourishment for the bitch when in her wild state, she had to stay in her lair after whelping. These after-births would provide nourishment to sustain her for several days. Furthermore, the after-birth contains essential vitamins and minerals which are absolutely essential to her. It also contains a substance which promotes the production of milk and this is why, if she is unlucky enough to have to have a Caesarian section, the veterinary surgeon will usually give you the after-birth to take home and give to the bitch.

There is no definite time between the birth of each puppy. Sometimes one will follow another with great rapidity. At other times there will be a long delay, sometimes running to an hour or two. While waiting, the bitch will lie quietly, resting and frequently licking the puppies she has, stimulating them to live and eat.

Almost always, at some time during the labour, there is a long delay. This usually turns out to be the 'half-way' mark. I do not mean that this pause will occur when exactly half the litter has been born, but when all the puppies from one horn of the uterus have been expelled. It is possible, but does not happen very often, that there is only one puppy in the second horn.

Whilst the whelping is actually taking place, the bitch may completely refuse to take anything to drink, but if she takes milk then that is good, and it should always be offered absolutely cold, since this will stimulate the whelping action; warm milk would be conducive to sleep.

When you think she has finally finished whelping, all bedding should be changed, the bitch settled with her babies, a drink of milk left with her in the box and she should be left to sleep.

A maiden bitch may not appear to have any milk at all, but almost certainly this will be produced as soon as the babies start suckling. However, if she does delay a bit don't worry too much, since a newborn puppy can well exist for a long time without food so long as it is kept warm.

The next three or four days are very important in the life of your litter. The bitch should be looked at every three or four hours, just to make sure that all is well, so that you will immediately spot a puppy which is being pushed away and so not getting his share of the milk-bar or is becoming chilled. You'll know as soon as you open the door of the whelping room, for then you should be met with either complete silence or with the wonderful sound of puppies suckling contentedly. Sometimes, you may hear hungry cries but this is probably because you have arrived at the start of feeding time when everyone is trying to get hold of a teat. However, there is one sound which really terrifies me. This is the cry which sounds like a young kitten mewing and this always denotes a hungry puppy which is weak and sickly and for which there is not very much to be done. However, such a puppy can be worked on and sometimes it survives. Take the puppy away, wrap it in a blanket and pop it in a very low oven, with the door ajar of course, and leave it there for a while. He can also, most effectively, be pushed down your neck inside your sweater, so long as you are wearing a belt, so that he cannot fall right through, and this way is the best of all, for he receives not only the warmth of your body but also all the movement as well while you go about your daily chores. Just a word of warning on taking a puppy away. Either do it when the mother is absent or else take two puppies, both in the same hand, then quickly slip one out of sight and the other back to mum.

There is just one other thing I will warn you about. You may find, especially with a large litter, that some of the puppies are born with a curvature of the spine. Do not let this worry you, not even if it is quite bad. Such puppies do fine and usually by the time they are six weeks old, such a curvature has completely disappeared. I think it is due to lack of room in the uterus.

Continue to watch for a puppy being pushed away and if it is, then hold it on to the nipple for a definite period, at least 10 minutes every two hours, until it regains its strength and can fend for himself.

If, because of the size of the litter or for some other reason, the mother cannot care for them, then you have a task on your hands. It is perfectly possible, but it is hard work, to hand-rear a litter. In recent years a new method has been evolved. This is tube-feeding. It is absolutely ideal, especially if you have a whole litter to be hand-reared or where you have just one puppy which you want to help 'over the hump' while he cannot suckle properly. It is such a good idea because it is so time-saving.

You can obtain, from your veterinary surgeon or the chemist a tiny plastic tube, made especially for the purpose. This is placed in the puppy's mouth and so into its stomach, attached to a needle-less hypodermic syringe, then the milk is slowly and gently fed direct through the tube into the stomach. This may sound alarming, and for the first time, it is. However, the puppy quickly learns to swallow the tube and this can then be marked off, to show how much must be inside the puppy, before the syringe full of milk is attached. There is only one thing you must be certain of and that is that the tube is in the stomach and not in the lungs. This can be quickly established, before touching the plunger, because if, by bad luck, the tube has taken the wrong turning, bubbles will immediately show in the milk. The food is fed very slowly, but even so it is vastly more rapid than the old method of bottle feeding. However, do not always feed with the tube. If you are hand-rearing throughout the whole time and not just 'topping up' a puppy, I think that at least once in 24 hours you should return to bottle feeding since this gives the puppy extra stimulus which is of great benefit to him.

If you are using a bottle or tube feeding simply as a supplement then you do not have many problems because mother will completely care for the litter, but if you are feeding a litter which has no mother then you have much more to do. It is essential to keep the babies very warm and you must also do something to copy the motion of the mother's tongue on them. You must, after each feeding, rub their tummies gently in a circular motion with a piece of cotton wool dipped in olive oil, and continue until each puppy evacuates. They must be kept scrupulously clean, by wiping with cotton wool dipped into a mild antiseptic. Dettol is good, and care must be taken to dry them afterwards.

As soon as the puppies seem to be doing well, the space between feeds can be lengthened, until the babies are three weeks old, but before this time you should be able to allow them to go at least six hours overnight, feeding every four hours except for this one period. At three weeks start weaning them onto raw meat, and the usual weaning procedure should be followed.

You must keep the bottles, bowls, etc., sterilised and

the bottle or tube and teats if you are using them must be kept in cold water.

When the whelping has concluded, you will find your bitch most unwilling to leave her litter for the first day or two, and I never make one leave for the first 24 hours if she does not wish to do so, but then she must be encouraged to go out, even to stay away for about 10 minutes, if she will. No bitch should be allowed to take exercise for lengthy periods until she has completely finished with her babies, since too much excitement and exercise will cause the milk to dry up and it can cause calcium derangement.

For at least 24 hours after the last puppy is born, mother should have no solid food at all, being kept on milk and egg, Lactol and stock. If, at the end of the first day, she appears perfectly normal, a little solid food may be given, especially raw beef, but really a bitch is perfectly O.K. on liquids for 48 hours after whelping, and I only give meat in this period if the bitch turns against milky foods. It is also to her advantage to add a dessert-spoonful of glucose to her meal, twice daily.

Once the first two days are passed the bitch must be given all the food she will eat. I always put them back at once onto the prewhelping diet and, in addition, she has a bowl of milk always in her box with her, but she must always have fresh water as well. By doing this there is, of course, always a risk that she will tip it up, but I find she rarely does so, and by leaving it with her you will find she will almost certainly drink 4 – 5 pints of milk daily. If she has only had a tiny litter, then of course she will need less food, but if she has six or more babies she needs 2 – 3 lb [0.9 – 1.4 kg] of meat daily and do remember that nothing makes milk the way that raw meat does.

All Collies are born with dew-claws (the additional claw half-way up the leg) on the front legs. Very occasionally, you may find them on the hind legs also and these *must* be removed. However, it is up to you what you do about the front ones. Most people seem to leave them on, I always did so. If you do have rear ones then you should get your veterinary surgeon to remove them. It is a very simple task, but one which you should not attempt unless you have seen it done expertly first.

So your puppies are growing along nicely and there is nothing for you to do until they are three weeks old (even a little earlier if the bitch is young or the litter very large), when the time comes for weaning. The first meal should be one of scraped raw meat or raw paunch, very, very, finely minced, giving about one dessertspoonful per puppy. Of course, they must be fed separately and by hand to start with, but after two days I'm sure they will have learned how to manage things themselves. At this time they can have two meat meals daily, and a day or two later offer a third meal, but this time it should be a milky one, made of milk and Readybrek, or Farex if you can afford it. By the time you arrive at the beginning of the fifth week the puppies can be introduced to yet another meal, this time of one of the really good biscuit meals (Saval or Weetmeal I), very thoroughly soaked in boiling stock so that the meal doubles in volume, it should be covered and left to stand for at least four hours before use. Towards the end of this week yet another meal can be added. This can be any of our own breakfast cereals with milk and their own ration of Canoval or SA37. So now their rations are as follows:

Breakfast : Cereals with Canoval or SA37.
11.00 a.m.: 3 – 4 oz [85 – 113 g] raw meat.
 2.00 p.m.: Farex and milk.
 5.00 p.m.: 3 – 4 oz raw meat.
Bedtime   : Biscuit meal soaked in stock.

 would point out that the above diet sheet is for *each* puppy.

As soon as you start feeding the babies, mother can stay away from them for longer periods, until by five weeks she is only with them at night, if at all! She may prefer to look in for a game night and morning. Except for the meat meals I have not given any guide as to size, since every puppy varies and it is left to you to work on it. Each day the size of meals can increase slightly, but do not give more than five meals. The five meals should be given until the babies are eight weeks of age, when they can be cut to four. After the first few days of weaning you no longer scrape the meat, and either chop or mince it instead. At six weeks my babies get their meat in one lump to tear and chew at and this goes on throughout their lives.

Very occasionally, when puppies first receive mixed feeding, they develop diarrhoea. This is not serious but must not be allowed to persist. You can give a meal of arrowroot and milk, or a dose (1 teaspoonful) of McLeans stomach powder.

All puppies have worms, that is a fact. Puppies should be wormed at about three weeks of age, then again at least once more before they are sold. Worm them on a dry day if you can, and one without wind, so there will be little chance of them catching a chill. The vermifuge should be obtained from your veterinary surgeon.

Many bitches, when their babies are about four weeks old, will start to regurgitate their part-digested food for them. This is an annoying but perfectly natural habit. The best thing to do is to feed her out of sight and sound of the babies: do not let her go back to them for three hours or so, preferably just after they have been fed.

It is terribly important, from the time the puppies are one week old, to cut their toe-nails, every week, for otherwise, they scratch their mother and this may well turn her against her litter. It is quite simple to do, just nipping off the sharp little points with a pair of scissors.

Now you have made your first big step, your litter has been reared successfully, and it's up to you to carry on, and hope there may be a Champion in that first litter.

Five: Puppy Rearing

From the age of about five weeks it is entirely your responsibility how the babies turn out.

Years of experience are needed to help you decide the pick of your litter, so it is a good idea to allow as many people as possible to see the litter whilst it is growing up. Of course, I mean people who have lots of experience in breeding Collies, particularly in the line in which your puppies are bred. Again, there is a big 'pro' in having a bitch on breeding terms because of course her owner will be as anxious as you to see the puppies and select them.

For myself, I like to pick my babies while they are still wet, then I don't want to make any further choice until the puppies are six months or more. This is not possible until you have bred a number of litters. Your puppy, picked while wet, will always be 'pick of litter'. It might be pick of a poor litter, it may be pick of an outstanding one, but he will always be the best; anyone who tells you that that wet puppy is a potential champion is quite mad!

Puppies are always born with pink noses, but these usually turn black very quickly; with a blue merle it takes longer, as it does where the white hair on the nose actually reaches to the end of the nose. Sometimes, with a blue merle, the pink patches take a very long time, sometimes as long as a year, to go black, but they almost always do, so be hopeful.

The puppies' eyes should be open on about the 10th – 14th days, if the puppies are born around the 63rd day. You must remember that the eyes really open on the 73rd day after conception, rather than after the date of birth, so a litter born early will take longer to open their eyes. If you do find a litter in which there is one puppy whose eyes are late to open it is a good plan to massage the eyelids very gently, with butter or olive oil. This makes the bitch lick the spot and the use of her tongue helps the eyes to open. When they first open the eyes are always blue and, to anyone experienced, there is a lot of difference in the colour. The eye which begins to change last of them all, will be the lightest eye. Of course, the blue eyes of the merle is yet again a different blue.

Of course you will have all the puppies to look after until they are six to seven weeks old, but then you should just have your special puppy to concentrate on. One of the most important things to do is to find some toys which will really occupy him. A rubber-ring, an old stocking knotted, and a big ball. I say big, because he must not be able to swallow it.

The five meals should be continued until the puppy is eight weeks, then they can be cut to four. These should be continued as long as the baby will accept them, specially during the winter months, but when they are cut to three, they should be:

Breakfast : Cereals with milk and the dose of Canoval or SA37 following instructions on the box, and an egg from time to time.

Early evening : 12 – 16 oz [340 – 454 g] of raw meat.

Bed-time : Bowl of biscuit meal soaked in stock.

These three meals should be continued until he is about eight to nine months, when his teething will be over and at this time he can go to two meals daily and remain on them for the rest of his life. During all his puppyhood he can be given big raw bones to chew and, of course, he must always have fresh water.

Not only must your puppy be well fed whilst he is growing up, but you must also ensure that his periods of exercise and sleep are correct. In his early months, the latter is more important than the former. He must have his own place where he can go whenever he feels tired and wants to sleep.

Correct ear-carriage is an essential part of all Collies.

If the ears are allowed to go up and stay there, your Collie is then ruined, since his lovely expression will have gone. Now is the time to watch and take action.

Until a puppy is around seven weeks old its ears are usually down on the side of his head, but around this age they assume the desired 'semi-erect' position. However, they very rarely keep the desired position! Ear-carriage varies from day to day, even hourly. If you find a puppy whose ears do not go up at all, it may be a good idea to shave them, but be careful, because you may finish with a prick-eared Collie. Never do any shaving before the puppy is 12 weeks of age. But a puppy who, at this age, has ears which stand up must be taken in hand at once, for once the ears are up they become hard and un-manageable and your battle is already lost. The prick-ear must never have weights put on it, this only strengthens the muscle, which fights against the weight and ends up in an ear which is even more strongly pricked than in the beginning. The most satisfactory method is to keep the ear-tip well greased. This is best done with kaolin, taking a fair-sized piece of it and rubbing it into the ear, to the top third only, then the greased part should be dipped into ash, from the fire, or very fine sand, to stop the grease getting onto your clothes and furniture. Kaolin contains glycerine, which keeps the ear soft. Continue with this treatment as long as necessary and when you want to remove it, do so with water and soap. Often an ear will go up later in life: when a bitch is in season, in whelp, when an adult casts his coat and often for no reason at all. The treatment is exactly the same.

At this stage of growing up a puppy has a great deal to do physically. In a very short time he must grow from a fluffy bundle to an elegant, graceful adult, a show dog we hope. He should be allowed to do this quietly. Do not try to fill him full of too many new ideas while he is undergoing this period of intensive growth. You must housetrain him, leash train him and, if you have a car, then car train him also, since the earlier he becomes used to travel the better. Except for these things do not demand much of him. Let him play, romp and gallop and, most important, *sleep*. Many, many Collies are ruined because the owners do not realise that the baby puppy needs as much sleep as the human baby. He cannot use his growing powers to their utmost unless he gets sleep.

There are a number of different views on grooming and it is up to you to decide how often your puppy is groomed. At this time it is only really a case of getting him used to the brush and comb, since there is not much but fluff to groom! But he must become accustomed to standing on the grooming table. He must also get used to noises, so never creep about around him – crash his feeding bowl etc. and make him associate the noise with his food.

Although a well-reared puppy will always be plump,

he still goes through a 'legs and wings' stage when you will be quite certain that he will never be fit for showing or anything! Provided he is well covered nothing else matters. Give him all he will take to eat, Collies are rarely terribly greedy and he will not over-eat; if he is well supplied with bone- and body-building foods, plenty of fresh water and a warm, dry place to sleep, plenty of exercise and lots of human companionship, you should be building up a really good Collie.

Rearing one puppy is not easy, so always try and make it two. They play and exercise together and provide competition at feeding time. You can always sell one when you no longer need him, if you are not, by then, too attached!

Rough Collie puppies at seven weeks old

A rolled-stitched leather collar

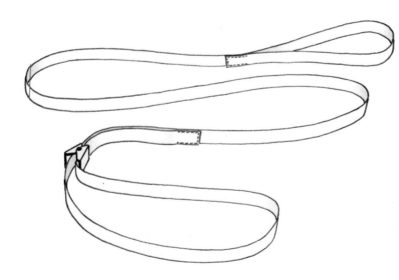

A nylon slip-lead

Six: Management

Even if the dog is your only one and will live in the house with you, he must still have his own bed to which he can go when he wants or to which he can be sent if necessary. He must have either a box into which he creeps or an open bed, on legs, anything which keeps him out of draughts. If a dog has no draught-free place to go he cannot be blamed for sitting on the sofa!

His exercise must be regular. He does not need hours of road work, but does best by being allowed to run free in fields, perfect when you have two dogs, since they exercise one another. If you have only one and cannot arrange a playmate for him it is essential really that you play ball with him or throw sticks for him, this will provide the galloping which he needs.

No dog should ever be exercised on the road without a leash. No matter how well trained he is, an accident can always happen and with the traffic as it is today one must not take risks. His collar should *never* be a chain choke, such a collar breaks the neck hair, and I am certain that, because the ears of a sheepherding dog are very sensitive, the noises made by such a collar reaches the point of cruelty. The correct collar is either a hand-rolled leather one, which can be either a choke collar or an ordinary one, or else a simple nylon choke collar.

Your dog should be exercised no matter what the weather. On hot days he should be exercised morning and evening. He comes to no harm if exercised in the rain and can be wiped down with a chamois when he gets home. Snow is his delight and this does present some problems with the balls of snow which form on their feathering and between his toes. These should be combed off as soon as he comes home.

Food is of the utmost importance, but today it is rather a different matter feeding the adult dog. There is such a

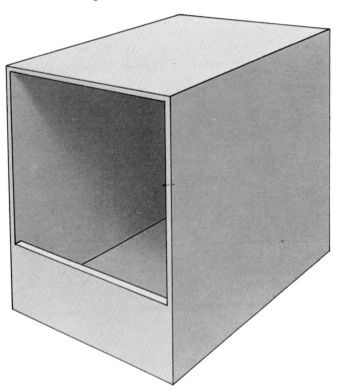

big variety of 'complete foods' on the market, that choosing is quite difficult. It is up to you.

Your dog should remain on two meals throughout his life. A breakfast of cereals and milk and the main meal. If you are choosing a complete food, then that is that, but if you prefer to give a varied diet and are feeding in the 'old fashioned' manner, then you have a fairly big, though pricey, diet to choose from. If you can get paunches then these are the best and cheapest. The average Collie requires $1 - 1\frac{1}{2}$ lb of meat daily, which can be given with a plain biscuit meal, soaked. Herrings, pricey nowadays, are good feed as are mackerel. He can have eggs, rabbit, chicken, tongue, heart etc., but all the offal should be cooked, except liver from a human consumption dealer. Pig's trotters are excellent food, since they make a wonderful thick, rich stock. Bones may be fed, but should always be fed raw. Cooked bones splinter and become dangerous. Poultry bones should never be given. If you are soaking meal, this must be done carefully. Various meals absorb different quantities of stock.

The adult Rough Collie needs two meals per day

It is necessary to add just sufficient to make the meal absorb it and turn into a dryish, crumbly food. The stock must always be added at about boiling point, covered and left to cool. Half-soaked meal will cause indigestion, over-soaked is usually unpalatable.

The Collie, because he has a long history of close association with man, needs plently of love and human companionship. From this comes his training. The untrained dog is a nuisance to everyone. Every dog, like every child, needs and is better for discipline. Every puppy learns his name first of all. This is usually no problem, the constant association of his name with his food, teaches this in no time. Once he has this name well established then further training takes place.

The first thing he must learn is to come when he is called. With this, except for bursts of high-spirited disobedience, you should have no trouble. The great thing is never to allow him to get away with refusing to come. This is, perhaps, the most trying exercise to overcome if he shows bursts of disobedience. He must *always* be praised when he does come, even if it is after a long delay. Remember that once he has been called, he has *got* to come and when he does he must be rewarded. You must *never* beat him after he has come, because, to his way of thinking, he has come and will most certainly associate punishment with having come – he cannot reason that he is being scolded for the time he took to arrive. If once you scold him when he comes, you have only yourself to blame if he never comes again.

At the age of about 8 – 10 weeks he must be taught to walk on a leash. The best leash to use for this is a nylon slip. But be quite certain that the leash is on the right way round (see diagram). For the very first lesson it does not matter at all in which direction he goes, just as long as he does go. It is essential for this lesson that he is quite alone, for you will need his full attention. Once the leash is on, and he moves, go with him. This is the easiest way to teach him that things are not too bad and after a short time of 'go where you like' the puppy will be ready and willing to come with you when you call his name. Don't forget to talk reassuringly to him and to praise him inordinately when he trots along.

All lessons should be short, a matter of minutes only, but this lesson must be learned before it is given up, he must at least be walking *his* way with the lead on. With this exception, lessons should rarely last more than five minutes for the very young puppy.

Having taught him to come when called and walk on

the lead, his further lessons will follow simply, sit and lie down, and there is little else he will need just to be a companion. These too, are simple to teach, but please remember never to change your word of command. Be consistent, never lose you temper, keep the word of the command simple and always precede it with his name. Don't use the word 'down' today and 'lie down' tomorrow, it will only confuse.

The youngster must get used to seeing and being handled by strangers from an early age; so his faith in people will develop. He must become used to strange noises and to traffic. Take him out on a busy road from time to time, to let him see the world.

There remains just the question of house-training and, since Collies are so clean, this rarely presents any difficulty. Common sense is all that is needed. He must

Kennel and run plan showing one section with a safety gate
The size of the kennel should not be less than 6 feet (1.8 metres) × 4 feet (1.2 metres) and the adjoining run should not be less than 8 feet (2.4 metres) × 6 feet (1.8 metres)

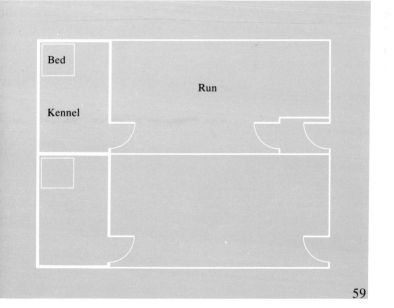

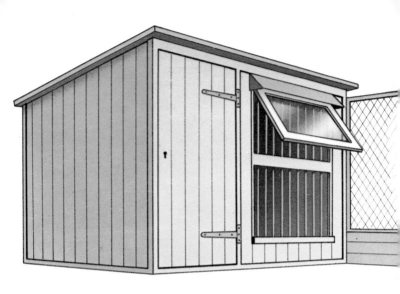

An outside proprietary kennel

An outdoor puppy pen should provide shelter and water

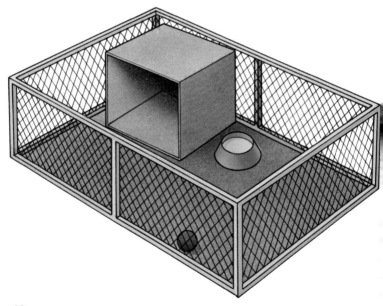

60

always be taken to the same place when he is put out. He will want to relieve himself immediately after a meal, so be ready to put him on the chosen spot. So too must he go to the same spot whenever he wakes. He must never be more than very gently scolded, if he makes a mistake. If he sleeps in the kitchen overnight, then he should have newspaper put down; gradually this can be moved nearer and nearer the door so that, when he can last all night, he will have learned that he must go outside.

There are at least two schools of thought on the subject of grooming. Groom daily or groom weekly. Either method is perfectly suitable for your dog. Grooming should mainly be done with a good brush only. Too

Grooming the Rough Collie: first turn the coat back, working from the rear, then thoroughly brush half-inch by half-inch (12 mm) towards the tail

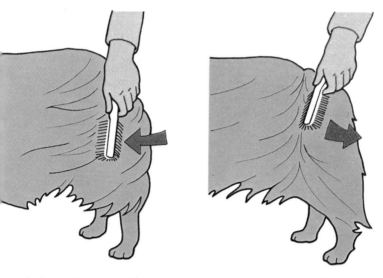

much combing spoils the coat and a comb is really only necessary when the coat is being cast. Then it must be got out, and as fast as possible, in order to give the new coat every opportunity of pushing through and coming as quickly as it can. At the time of moult, the dog should be

Wire pin brush

Oval bristle brush

Wooden-handled fine-toothed comb

Metal-handled coarse-toothed comb

Double rounded scissors

Trimming scissors

Nail clippers

Guillotine type nail clippers

Dental scaler

combed daily, even if your usual programme is a weekly one. Your dog must be groomed right down to the skin, and the best kind of brush to use is a radial nylon one, the way the bristles penetrate is really excellent.

Whether your routine is daily or weekly, the plan is exactly the same. Start at the back end of your dog and make a kind of parting across the body, from side to side, brushing the hair both ways, towards the tail, and towards the head. Having done one strip of the body, continue in the same way advancing about one inch at a time until you have completed the entire body from tail root to ears. Then start on the sides, working from under the tummy towards the back-bone. Next to come are his legs and tail and finally his chest and head. The chest hair should be groomed upwards, towards the chin, and then gently downwards again, leaving the edges of the chest area in the upwards position. For the tail, groom it as usual and then brush the underneath tail hair the wrong way. Hold the tail in your hand while you brush out the feathering on the hindquarters, towards the sides, leaving a place to drop the tail into.

Seven: The Show

Undoubtedly, the day will come when someone talks you into showing your Collie. Your first thing then is to make sure he has some training for the show ring. Having carried out the ideas given to you earlier in this book, you will almost be there, but there are some little extras which you will find necessary. He may need extra experience in getting used to strange people and places, your local Woolworths or a fairly large railway station are ideal for extending his experience. One point also, don't forget he may be expected to walk up and down stairs, so make sure he has met them before in his life. If you live in a bungalow, find a friend who will let you teach your dog about stairs. Next, he must be taught to make the most of himself in the show ring. Firstly, he will be expected to walk on a loose lead. This is most important for a judge cannot assess his movement if he is pulling away, or if you are stringing him up so that his feet barely reach the floor. If you walk him once on a tight lead the judge will almost certainly give you a second chance, but if you fail this time I'm afraid the judge will not spare more time on you – he just cannot when he has big numbers of dogs to assess in the one day. A dog which is strung up is probably so held because he is shy and once his lead is loosened this becomes apparent. So give your dog confidence and make him used to trotting beside you on a loose lead, with his tail gently wagging. Don't forget also, that if you yourself lack confidence, or are rather shy, such nerves will be transmitted at once along the lead. As you gain confidence so will your dog show better and better.

As well as the loose lead he must be taught also to stand and show himself off to advantage. He must stand steadily and four-square taking up the position quite naturally. He should stop at the end of his walk and step

Table

"New" dogs (unseen by Judge)

Handler

Dog being examined by Judge

Judge

"Old" dogs (already seen by Judge in a previous class)

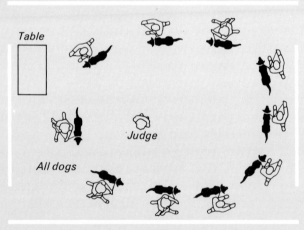

Table

Judge

All dogs

"Once round, please"

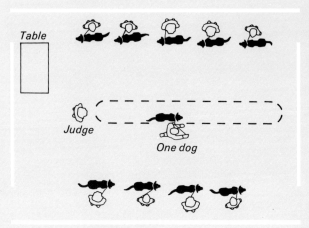

"Once up and down, please"

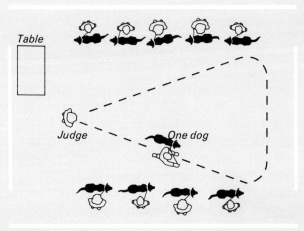

"Triangle, please"

67

into his position. While so standing, he must show off his ears for his chances may be lost if he is not showing them off to advantage when the judge turns round. How you do this will be a question of trial and error. He may like a little noise you can make, or a special tit-bit which you can secrete in your pocket, giving him a tiny piece from time to time. By the time he is six months old he should be having a daily, very short lesson never lasting more than five minutes. So now he walks beside you, always on your left and always alongside you. There is no reason why you cannot talk to him, quietly, to give him confidence and to hold his attention. This must go further, since he must walk beside you in a circle, always keeping to the left. In addition, he must learn to walk in an absolutely straight line, turn at the end and come back, still on the same line. Nowadays almost all judges ask you to walk in a triangle. This means walking away in a straight line, turning left at the end of the ring, then, in the corner, left again to bring you back right to the judge.

Considering how many judges ask for this, I am always surprised how many people look as if it was a big surprise, and the peculiar shapes of some of these 'triangles' never cease to astonish me! At the end of this triangle he must walk into his position to show himself off. He will do this to a word of command, so watch him and see his feet are correct, turned neither in nor out, and not too close together nor too far apart. These things can be put right by asking him to take another step. So there he stands, head up, ears alert looking a king. But there is a chance that he may 'settle down'. By this I mean that, though still standing, he becomes a little slack, his neck sinks into his shoulders, his elbows spreading and his whole body settling down. This must be checked. He must not be allowed to try and sit down either, just take a pace, or even half of one, to set him up again. All this must be done quite unobtrusively, so as not to draw the judge's attention to a possible fault.

Our Collies require little or no stripping as show preparation. Provided the coat is always well groomed, free from tangles and mats, free of foreign bodies, live or otherwise, there is little to do, except for a good, final grooming. It is not necessary to bath a Collie, but his white parts may be washed, though his legs may be the only part which really needs this. This should be done the day before the show: the dog partially dried, his coat then filled with chalk or one of the cleaning powders. If these preparations are put into a damp coat they will stay there, and should be left, until you have arrived at the show before being groomed out. No chalk may be in the coat in the show ring. This is a Kennel Club ruling.

A bit of attention to the legs and feet is necessary. The feet should be trimmed all round so that the hair is cut level with the foot itself, giving a clear outline. Further, the hair between the toes should be cut away, this area should be kept clear of hair at all times, since it tends to spread the foot if it is left packed with hair. The hair below the hock is trimmed right off, with scissors. The only other part which, in this country, is trimmed, are the ears. Any long, wispy hair should be removed, but the ear should not be trimmed with scissors, since this gives a hard impression and quite spoils the soft, sweet expression we are seeking.

The best thing is for you to subscribe to one of the dog papers, *Dog World* or *Our Dogs*, for these usually carry advertisements for shows and you will find what you want.

Having decided on your show, make your entries, and then be off. It is best to choose a local show, since this makes everything much easier for you. At such a show you may find there are no classes for Collies and you can only enter in Variety classes. If you are simply looking on your outing as one to obtain experience, don't let this worry you, you may find the judge is not very knowledgeable about Collies, but this does not matter since you want experience. But if you find a show where there are classes for the breed, then so much the better and let us hope the judge is really an acknowledged expert on the breed; here you will learn a great deal, even if you do not win.

Before you can make your entries the dog must, of course, have been registered with the Kennel Club. This will probably have been done before you received him so it remains for you to transfer him. This you do by sending the appropriate form, with the fee of £3.00 to the Kennel Club. You need not wait to receive it back before entering, but it must have been sent.

Having made your entries all that remains is to go, taking with you his grooming tools, a blanket for him to lie on, since the show will almost certainly be unbenched and he will want somewhere to lie.

It will have been best if you have entered him in two

classes at least, since, at his first show, he may need a class in which to settle down. Too many classes may make him bored, so choose the happy medium.

I hope you have arrived early in order to find a place where you can bed-down the Collie before the crush of exhibitors arrive. Then start on the final grooming, getting rid of any chalk you may have left in his coat and then, at the last moment, doing the last titivations. Now you are ready for your first class. Find out where and when Collies will be judged. Every ring, in addition to the judge, has one or more stewards. These are men or women who, from sheer love of the sport, act in a purely voluntary capacity, giving their services to help you on your way, so please never be rude to a steward. The steward will notify exhibitors before the first class, that Collies are about to be judged, but it is entirely up to you to be in the ring at the correct moment. When you go into the ring for your first class, the steward who is marshalling the dogs gives you your ring number, this you must wear to identify your dog. When you are all assembled, judging begins. Usually the judge asks you all to walk around the ring together. This gives him a chance to look at the dogs and usually gives a good judge an idea of which dogs are likely to figure among the winners. For this you must go round in an anti-clockwise manner, with the dogs on your *inside*. Always be sure your dog is between you and the judge. He will stop you when he has seen enough and begin his individual judging. He goes over each dog, one by one, usually he starts with an overall impression, gained when you stand him in the centre of the ring, using his ears and making the most of himself, so you see how necessary it is that your dog is trained since the judge cannot waste time, he usually spends about 90 seconds on a dog. Then he will look at him bit by bit, his teeth, his head, his eyes, his body, legs, tail and coat. Then he moves you along, and

this is a very important moment, because a lot can be learned from this moving. Although the judge cannot waste time on you, he will usually be as helpful as he possibly can, specially to the novice exhibitor. The exhibitor should never speak to the judge, except to answer a question. You are usually asked to tell his age, that is all. The least said in the ring the better, for even the best intentioned remarks will be bound to cause unfavourable comment from the other exhibitors.

The judge will then indicate to you that he has finished with you for the time being, and you will return, either to your original place, or to the end of the line, the steward will tell you. If it is your first show, tell the steward so before you start, he will then keep a special eye on you.

72

The judge then goes over each dog in the class and, while he is doing so, let your dog rest. He can sit or lie down if he wants to. Keep an eye on the judge though and, when he is examining the one before the last, wake your dog up and get him ready to show again. The judge will then go back down the ring, looking at each dog in turn. Then he pulls out about half a dozen, and often at this stage dismisses the others. Then he makes his final decisions from the remaining dogs, gives out the prize cards, and that class is finished. If you are entered in the next class, you will not leave the ring but will stand apart from the new dogs which come in, until the judge has examined them, then you will be considered with the new ones, and again the cards will be given out. Let us imagine that you were placed third or fourth in your first class and that the class was 'Puppy'. The next class may be Maiden or Novice, and it is possible that the winners of the Puppy Class are not eligible for the Maiden Class, so you might well find yourself placed second, even first. When he has judged all his classes, all the first prize winners are called into the ring together and from these first prize winners, the judge will choose the Best of Breed. Then, the winner of Best of Breed goes on, probably under another judge, to compete for Best in Show. If you have won Best of Breed you are only eligible for Best in Show if you have not been shown in Variety classes, or have been shown and won those classes as well. Something you dare not hope for at your very first shows!

Eight: Accidents and other Problems

Happily, the Collie is not usually afflicted by many of the complaints which afflict other breeds – canker etc. – however, you must always be ready for an accident, so have a medicine chest ready and handy. Most of the items you need will be found in an ordinary household chest.

Sprains and Bruises: A dog, especially a puppy, may often hurt himself when he is playing and, on rushing to examine the reason for a wild scream of pain, you will find him dead lame – so badly so that he will tell you he will certainly never walk again! Take him away from his companions and put him somewhere without a slippery floor (not on lino) and leave him alone until, of his own accord, he finds his feet again. He will often be quite O.K. again in as little as 30 minutes and will be yelling to rejoin his companions.

However, if the sprain or bruise seems more serious, then something must be done. I have great faith in a homeopathic remedy. Soak a pad of cotton wool in water and squeeze dry, then soak it again in tincture of Arnica flowers, do not squeeze it, but apply to the injured spot, so long as the skin is not broken, and bandage lightly. It is a good thing to put a piece of plastic over the pad and under the bandage. It is pretty certain the puppy will try to get the bandage off, so paint the outside with mustard, which not too many dogs like! The same treatment is equally good for adults. Although the bottle of tincture of Arnica bears the word 'poison', do not be afraid to dose the animal twice every day with a dessertspoonful of water to which 2 – 4 drops of tincture of Arnica have been added. This dosage is perfectly safe and works wonders.

If a dog tries to chew and tear at his bandages as if they were hurting him, this may well be the case. They may have been put on a little too tight, or the injury may have swollen later, causing the bandage to tighten. Make quite certain that this is not the case. Only when you are quite sure about this should you apply mustard or other 'off-putting' repellent, such as tincture of ginger or bitter aloes.

As an alternative way of treating bruises when the skin is broken, even grazed, you should, as soon as possible after the injury, bathe it well in icy water; this helps stop any bleeding below the skin and so reduces swelling. A few hours after his injury, wash again with hot water to stimulate the circulation and so help to disperse the results of the damage from the bruising.

Choking is something which quite often happens to your puppies. A dog approached by a strange dog, while he is eating, may bolt what ever is in his mouth. Many dogs, if not properly trained, will try and swallow any 'find' they may have made rather than give it up for inspection when asked to do so. Puppies can even bolt a ball if it is small enough, which is why I have said only give him big ones to play with.

If the object lodges in the upper part of the throat *action* must be the word, for the dog can suffocate in a very, very short time if his breathing is cut off. Open his mouth, don't worry if he tries to bite, but try to catch hold of the object and pull it up. If it will not come up, try and push it down gently. If the object goes to the lower part of the gullet, the immediate risk of death is over. You may have to have the object surgically removed afterwards, but your vet will decide this and at least your dog is alive.

Shock will follow almost any injury. The dog appears dazed and silly; in advanced cases he can lose consciousness. He becomes cold to the touch and his breathing is rapid and shallow and the inside of his mouth and eyelids appear pale. Try to get him to take a warm drink, if he is conscious. To this drink add lots of glucose and, failing that, sugar. Wrap him in a blanket and try to keep him warm.

Burns and Scalds: Shock always follows these two accidents and can often be severe. Unless the damage is very slight, never attempt to treat it yourself. Cover the injured area very lightly with a bandage, or, if it is over a large area, wrap the dog completely in a sheet, then in a blanket and get him to a veterinary surgeon immediately. You must try to keep air out of the injured area and treat for severe shock. Do not put any kind of medication on the burn. Scalds are more difficult to treat, because of the Collies' thick coat which holds the hot liquids to the skin. The best method is to douche the area with lukewarm water (never cold since this increases the shock) as a first measure. Burns and scalds which only cover a tiny area, can be treated with a paste of bicarbonate of soda (baking soda) and water. Spread it thickly on the area and make sure the dog does not lick it off.

Diarrhoea: This is usually a puppy complaint and is caused by a variety of reasons. In a case of diarrhoea castor oil should never be given. Liquid paraffin, however, is very good and may well remove the irritation which is causing the condition. Liquid paraffin is soothing as well as an aperient. Most usually diahorroea is caused by a chill or a sudden change of diet. He may respond to treatment which is only a bland diet or the administration of chlorodyne, 10 drops in half a teaspoonful of water, every four hours

Diarrhoea occurs in adults also and is rather more serious since it is often an early symptom of a virus or bacterial disease and the dog has, usually, a rise in temperature at the same time.

Eczema: This is a disease which does not often develop in Collies in Great Britain but it is often met with in the U.S.A. where it is called 'hot spots'. It is not contagious and is frequently seasonal. Two forms of eczema can be encountered, wet and dry, and neither of them is confined to any special area of the body. Moist eczema can appear in a matter of minutes. Quite often you put a perfectly fit, healthy dog to bed and wake up to encounter one which has a patch as big as a saucer, glistening, red, damp and completely hairless. These areas are very sensitive to the touch and are clearly symptomatic of the condition. Moist eczema frequently responds to treatment with calamine lotion, and you should try this before taking the dog for advice. The dog should be given a raw meat diet, plus the addition of raw tomatoes since the condition is caused by a deficiency of vitamin C, which is found in tomatoes, green vegetables, fruit etc.

Dry eczema is also not contagious, but it is very difficult to differentiate between the lesions of this condition and those of sarcoptic or follicular mange, both of which are highly contagious. You should take immediate professional advice if your dog has scaley patches on the body. Only a microscopic examination of scrapings can reveal the presence of the sarcopt or demodect and this is the main distinguishing feature between dry eczema and mange.

Many dogs will eat finely chopped lettuce when available, and this is good. Vitamin C can also be given in tablet form and is of great help in treating skin disease and septic wounds.

Enteritis (inflammation of the bowel): This is a serious condition. It is often accompanied by a very high temperature together with a loss of appetite, vomiting and thirst. However, sometimes the temperature is of no more than 102° – 104°F. Enteritis usually accompanies a specific disease, but it can be caused by worms, chills, decomposed foodstuffs, irritant poisons and swallowing of foreign bodies. Your dog must *never* be given any purgatives. The treatment is warmth and rest. The dog should not be given any solid food in the early stages but he can have liquids such as egg and milk, milk, barley water, groats, glucose and water or arrowroot gruel. If vomiting a great deal then he should only have barley water. A dose of liquid paraffin can be given but no other purgative and if the condition does not improve, you should ask your veterinary surgeon to see the dog.

Eye Injuries: These fairly frequently occur, either to a puppy by a puppy, or to an adult at exercise or work. Immediately an injury is noticed the cause must be looked for. It may be a grass seed in the eye, or any other similar object. This should be removed at once and the eye bathed with a boracic acid solution or with cold tea (no milk). An eye can easily be scratched and probably the best treatment is to put in some penicillin eye ointment. If bathing the eye before using the ointment, the eye should be bathed only with warm water, since the action of any chemical, i.e. boracic, might inhibit the action of the penicillin.

Foreign Bodies in the Eye: When trying to wash out a foreign body from the eye, hold the head on one side, raise the lower eyelid so that it makes a tiny cup, flood this with lukewarm water then let the dog's head go so that he can blink and the water washes round the eyeball. This will usually wash out a grass seed or a bit of grit. However, if this does not succeed, do not try any other treatment, put a spot of liquid paraffin in the eye and take your dog to a veterinary surgeon as soon as possible.

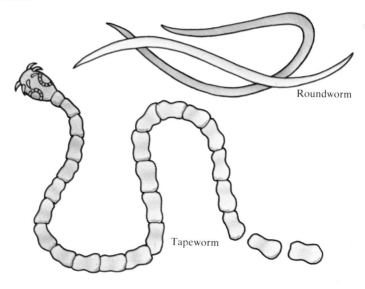

Roundworm

Tapeworm

Adult flea

Biting louse

Engorged female tick

Mite (microscopic)

Sucking louse

Stings: Since dogs tend to chase anything that comes into their vision they are often stung by wasps or bees. A bee leaves its sting in the skin, a wasp rarely does so. You probably will not have seen the accident take place, but if your dog comes to you with a badly swollen face or other part of the anatomy, and a sting is suspected, look for the centre of the swelling and if you can see a sting lodged there it is easy to remove with tweezers. You can then put a blue bag or half an onion on the spot. Do not use the blue bag inside the mouth. Alternatively the place can be treated with a paste of bicarbonate of soda and water, or you can put it on dry. Watch your dog carefully for a while to make sure the swelling is not increasing, for it is possible, though uncommon, for a dog to be suffocated by the presence of a swelling from a sting in the throat.

Urticaria (nettle rash): This is frequently met with and may be confused with a sting, for the dog appears swollen. However, the raised spots are flat and vary in size from a pea to a 50 pence piece. There are no scabs and no irritation and, in our breed (unless the condition appears on the face and legs), it is difficult to spot, but on the short-haired areas the hairs stand straight out. Urticaria is caused by internal toxicity and an adult Collie should receive a good half-teaspoonful of Epsom salts. One dose is usually sufficient. The dog should be kept on a laxative diet for a few days. If the condition remains or recurs in the same dog look for something in the diet to which the dog is sensitive and of course do not use it again.

Parasites: Worms have already been dealt with, so here we'll have a look at all the others. Many dogs, however well cared for, at some time in their lives will pick up a *flea* or two. These must be kept well controlled. Today that is easy since there are sprays available from your veterinary surgeon which kill the little blighters in no time at all. *Lice* are small bluish-grey insects which attach themselves to the skin and suck the blood of the dog. The most effective remedy is to bath the dog in a good insecticidal shampoo, but it is essential to see that the coat is soaked right down to the skin – not easy in a full-coated Collie – and the shampoo left in contact with the skin for about 15 minutes before rinsing. During this time you should continue shampooing and keep up friction so that your dog does not become chilled. The coat is then rinsed and the dog dried off. Alternatively, a powder can be used, but this must be repeated every fourth day five or six times, since the first powdering only kills the lice and does not touch the nits which continue to develop. *Harvest mites* are tiny little orange-coloured insects with the same habits as lice. As their name denotes they are usually found in the late summer and autumn and it is rare to find them except between the toes and occasionally round the eyes. The treatment again is an insecticidal shampoo or a blow with a powder. *Ticks:* country dogs will almost always, at some time in their lives, collect a tick. These attach themselves to the dog where they suck the blood and grow. When you find a tick do not pull it off, because in that way you will probably take the head only and the rest of the animal will cause a nasty sore. When you find it, put a drop of methylated spirit on it and after a few seconds try to pull it off gently with tweezers. If it will not come leave it to drop off naturally. If a tick fixes onto a dog's lip or eyelid, or if the dog is very upset, then you had better consult your veterinary surgeon. In some countries, ticks can carry a disease which causes paralysis, but, thank goodness, these diseases do not exist in this country.

Everyone must learn how to take a temperature. You must have a 'stumpy'-ended clinical thermometer, that is, one in which the end which holds the mercury is thick and rounded. The dog's normal temperature is 101.5°F. To take the temperature, you should lightly grease the end of the thermometer with Vaseline and insert it into the rectum, at a slight upward angle, keeping hold of it all the time it is in. Leave it there for one minute. Do not use force in inserting it and if there is any difficulty in inserting it, move it slightly. Don't forget, before using it, to check that it is well shaken down, at least to 96°F.

If the temperature is above normal, keep the dog under observation for a while. Never take the temperature immediately after play or exercise, for this may raise it by several degrees. At least an hour should elapse after exercise before a true reading can be obtained. If it is over 102°F rest a further hour then recheck. Some dogs, especially young ones, take a time to settle down.

The 'old wives' tale' that a dog with a wet, cold nose is a healthy dog and the one with a dry, hot nose is sick, is just a load of rubbish, except of course, when it is in a state of discharging mucus. A young puppy may run a temperature for no reason at all, and quite often he will have a rise in temperature during teething. But it is wise, if the temperature persists for more than 12 hours, to let your vet have a look.

The Smooth Collie

Nine: The Smooth Collie

The Smooth Collie is not a separate breed, but is exactly the same as the Rough, except for his coat, which is short and smooth, like the coat of a Dachshund.

He is the same typical Collie and often is really structurally better than the Rough because you simply cannot hide a fault in the ring. Some faults of body are often concealed by the coat and careful handling can keep them concealed from the judge. However, you cannot do this with a Smooth, everything is on display so he must have near faultless conformation. He requires great spring of rib, plenty of heart room and his quarters must be well turned and his shoulder well layed back. If he fails in any of these points they stand out immediately, so it is fairly certain that we will only find a sound dog in the Smooth Collie ring.

Sadly, the Rough has always been way ahead of the Smooth in numbers, because the Smooth has never been very popular, which is a great pity, since the ease of keeping him should certainly be an added reason for choosing a Smooth. It can only be the lovely coat of the Rough which makes him so popular, because in all other respects he is identical. Even today, the Smooth carries a big proportion of the blood of the Roughs, as the Kennel Club quite rightly permits the crossing of the two kinds of coat in this breed. In fact, practically all through their history, such a crossing was permitted, but it was in the early years of this century that the Smooth was at its peak and when the strains were more clearly defined. But even in those days the Roughs played a big part, and the outstanding Smooth of that period, Ch. Canute Perfection was by the Rough dog, Count of Moreton.

On several occasions the Smooth has been near extinction. After both the wars things were in a very sad state. Each time a little band of enthusiasts saved the breed. At those times it was essential to use the Rough in the matings, but you should realise that such a crossing never produces 'half-coated' puppies, they are always either Rough or Smooth. Such puppies can be registered in the breed to which they most nearly conform.

Many Smooths have carried the Collie to the top in the show ring, but the most outstanding of these was the lovely blue merle bitch, Ch. Laund Lynne. She was truly a picture, standing in the ring with her eyes fixed on her owner, Mr W. Stansfield, with every part of her quite rigid, except the very tip of her tail which gently moved from side to side. Many big awards came her way but the most important of these was, undoubtedly, the winning in the 1920s of the award for Best Non-Sporting exhibit in show at the Kennel Club's own Championship Show.

There is a slight increase in numbers of the breed today, but we still await the birth of another Laund Lynne!

FURTHER READING LIST

BOOKS

General

Glover, Harry (Ed.) *A standard guide to pure-bred dogs.* London, 1977.
Gordon, J. *Dogs.* Edinburgh, 1976.
Gould, Jean. *All about dog breeding for quality and soundness.* London, 1978.
Sutton, Catherine G. *The Observer's book of dogs.* London, 1978.
White, Kay. *Dog Breeding: A Guide to Mating & Whelping.* Edinburgh, 1980.

Specific

Bishop, Ada L. *All about the Collie* (2E). London, 1980.
Osborne, Margaret. *The Collie* (9E). London, 1978.

MAGAZINES

Australia

Australasian Kennel Review and Dog News,
Leader Publishing Company,
2 Dale Street,
Brookvale,
NEW SOUTH WALES 2100

Great Britain

Dog News and Family Pets,
National Dog Owner's Association,
92 High Street,
Lee on Solent,
Hampshire

Dog World,
22 New Street,
Ashford,
Kent

Our Dogs,
5 Oxford Road, Station Approach,
Manchester 1

United States of America

Bloodlines,
United Kennel Club Incorporated,
321 West Cedar Street,
Kalamazoo,
MI 49006

Collie Shetland Sheepdog Review,
M D Drucker,
8760 Appian Way,
Los Angeles,
CA 90046

Pure Bred Dogs (The American Kennel Club Gazette),
51 Madison Avenue,
New York,
NY 10010

USEFUL ADDRESSES

There are many clubs catering for different dog breeds. For your nearest clubs, addresses can be obtained from the main local branch of any kennel club.

Great Britain

The Kennel Club,
1 Clarges Street,
Piccadilly,
London W1Y 8AB

United States of America

The American Kennel Club,
51 Madison Avenue,
New York,
NY 10010

INDEX

Page numbers in italics refer to illustrations